The Essential B

C000271356

Choosing, Using & Maintaining your

ELECTRIC BICYCLE

Your expert:
Peter Henshaw

VELOCE PUBLISHING
THE PUBLISHER OF FINE AUTOMOTIVE BOOKS

Essential Buyer's Guide Series

Alfa Romeo Giulia GT Coupé (Booker)
Alfa Romeo Giulia Spider (Booker)
Audi TT (Davies)
Austin Seven (Barker)
Big Healeys (Trummel)
BMW E21 3 Series (1975-1983) (Cook & Reverente)
BMW E30 3 Series (1981 to 1994) (Hosier)
BMW GS (Henshaw)
BMW X5 (Saunders)
BSA 350 & 500 Unit Construction Singles (Henshaw)
BSA 500 & 650 Twins (Henshaw)
BSA Bantam (Henshaw)
Citroën 2CV (Paxton)
Citroën ID & DS (Heilig)
Cobra Replicas (Ayre)
Corvette C2 Sting Ray 1963-1967 (Falconer)
Ducati Bevel Twins (Falloon)
Ducati Desmodue Twins (Falloon)
Ducati Desmoquattro Twins – 851, 888, 916, 996, 998, ST4 1988 to 2004 (Falloon)
Fiat 500 & 600 (Bobbitt)
Ford Capri (Paxton)
Ford Escort Mk1 & Mk2 (Williamson)
Ford Mustang – First Generation 1964 to 1973 (Cook)
Ford Mustang – Fifth generation/S197 (Cook)
Ford RS Cosworth Sierra & Escort (Williamson)
Harley-Davidson Big Twins (Henshaw)
Hinckley Triumph triples & fours 750, 900, 955, 1000, 1050, 1200 – 1991-2009 (Henshaw)
Honda CBR FireBlade (Henshaw)
Honda CBR600 Hurricane (Henshaw)
Honda SOHC Fours 1969-1984 (Henshaw)
Jaguar E-Type 3.8 & 4.2-litre (Crespin)
Jaguar E-type V12 5.3-litre (Crespin)
Jaguar Mark 1 & 2 (All models including Daimler 2.5-litre V8) 1955 to 1969 (Thorley)
Jaguar S-Type – 1999 to 2007 (Thorley)
Jaguar X-Type – 2001 to 2009 (Thorley)
Jaguar XJ-S (Crespin)
Jaguar XJ6, XJ8 & XJR (Thorley)
Jaguar XK 120, 140 & 150 (Thorley)
Jaguar XK8 & XKR (1996-2005) (Thorley)
Jaguar/Daimler XJ 1994-2003 (Crespin)
Jaguar/Daimler XJ40 (Crespin)
Jaguar/Daimler XJ6, XJ12 & Sovereign (Crespin)
Kawasaki Z1 & Z900 (Orritt)
Land Rover Series I, II & IIA (Thurman)
Land Rover Series III (Thurman)
Lotus Seven replicas & Caterham 7: 1973-2013 (Hawkins)
Mazda MX-5 Miata (Mk1 1989-97 & Mk2 98-2001) (Crook)

Mazda RX-8 All models 2003 to 2012 (Parish)
Mercedes Benz Pagoda 230SL, 250SL & 280SL roadsters & coupès (Bass)
Mercedes-Benz 280-560SL & SLC (Bass)
Mercedes-Benz SL R129 Series (Parish)
Mercedes-Benz W124 – All models 1984-1997 (Zoporowski)
MG Midget & A-H Sprite (Horler)
MG TD, TF & TF1500 (Jones)
MGA 1955-1962 (Crosier)
MGB & MGB GT (Williams)
MGF & MG TF (Hawkins)
Mini (Paxton)
Morris Minor & 1000 (Newell)
Moto Guzzi 2-valve big twins (Falloon)
New Mini (Collins)
Norton Commando (Henshaw)
Peugeot 205 GTI (Blackburn)
Porsche 911 (964) (Streather)
Porsche 911 (993) (Streather)
Porsche 911 (996) (Streather)
Porsche 911 (997) Model years 2004 to 2009 (Streather)
Porsche 911 (997) Second generation models 2009 to 2012 (Streather)
Porsche 911 Carrera 3.2 (Streather)
Porsche 911 SC (Streather)
Porsche 924 – All models 1976 to 1988 (Hodgkins)
Porsche 928 (Hemmings)
Porsche 930 Turbo & 911 (930) Turbo (Streather)
Porsche 944 (Higgins)
Porsche 986 Boxster (Streather)
Porsche 987 Boxster & Cayman (Streather)
Rolls-Royce Silver Shadow & Bentley T-Series (Bobbitt)
Royal Enfield Bullet (Henshaw)
Subaru Impreza (Hobbs)
Sunbeam Alpine (Barker)
Triumph 350 & 500 Twins (Henshaw)
Triumph Bonneville (Henshaw)
Triumph Herald & Vitesse (Davies)
Triumph Spitfire & GT6 (Baugues)
Triumph Stag (Mort)
Triumph Thunderbird, Trophy & Tiger (Henshaw)
Triumph TR6 (Williams)
Triumph TR7 & TR8 (Williams)
Velocette 350 & 500 Singles (Henshaw)
Vespa Scooters – Classic 2-stroke models 1960-2008 (Paxton)
Volvo 700/900 Series (Beavis)
VW Beetle (Cservenka & Copping)
VW Bus (Cservenka & Copping)
VW Golf GTI (Cservenka & Copping)

www.veloce.co.uk

For post publication news, updates and amendments relating to this book please visit www.veloce.co.uk/books/V4939

First published in August 2016 by Veloce Publishing Limited, Veloce House, Parkway Farm Business Park, Middle Farm Way, Poundbury, Dorchester, Dorset, DT1 3AR, England.
Fax 01305 250479/e-mail info@veloce.co.uk/web www.veloce.co.uk or www.velocebooks.com.
ISBN: 978-1-845849-39-9 UPC: 6-36847-04939-3
Readers with ideas for automotive books, or books on other transport or related hobby subjects, are invited to write to the editorial director of Veloce Publishing at the above address.
British Library Cataloguing in Publication Data – A catalogue record for this book is available from the British Library.
Typesetting, design and page make-up all by Veloce Publishing Ltd on Apple Mac. Printed in India by Replika Press.

Contents

1 Introduction
– the purpose of this book

If you've never ridden an electric bicycle before, but are thinking about buying one, then you're in for a treat. Quite simply, they take a lot of the effort out of cycling. With their small electric motors and batteries, electric bikes help you cruise up hills and into headwinds. The first time you ride one, it feels like you've been endowed with supercharged legs!

Electric bikes, or 'pedelecs' (pedal-electric) as they're sometimes known, are a relatively new idea, but a good one.

So, how long does the battery last? Do you need a licence? Are they safe? Should you buy a complete electric bike, or just a conversion kit? This book answers all of these

Electric bikes make cycling easy ...

... but still bring a sense of achievement.

You don't need specialised clothing to ride an electric bike.

Power at your fingertip ...

questions and more, using straightforward, jargon-free language. It doesn't tell you which bike to buy, but it does describe what's available, and what might suit you best. It takes you through the advantages and pitfalls of owning an electric bike, the laws surrounding them, as well as how to look after your bike and get the most out of it.

The best thing about electric bikes is their simplicity: these really are bicycles with a little extra power added, so they're very easy to ride and use

It's official: electric bikes are cool.

very little energy. Perhaps, in a world of finite resources, that's just what we need. Not only that, but they're also great fun. Enjoy!

Acknowledgements

Thanks go David Henshaw at A to B for his help with pictures: www.atob.org.uk provides a regularly updated price list of all electric bikes on sale in Britain. Thanks also to all the importers who provided pictures, to Anna Finch, and to Riley's Cycles, Sherborne, for advice on electric bike kits.

Essential Buyer's Guide™ currency

At the time of publication, a BG unit of currency "●" equals approximately £1.00/US$1.47/Euro 1.30. Please adjust to suit current exchange rates using Sterling as the base currency.

2 FAQs
– making sure you're informed

Are they easy to ride?

Yes. If you can ride a standard pedal cycle, you can ride an electric bike. Apart from bikes with a separate throttle (see page 52), it's just a case of pedalling: the power comes in automatically (see page 53).

Do I need a licence?

No. Falling within the EU power and speed limits, these are bicycles in the eyes of the law (see page 17), so you don't need a licence, insurance, an MoT, to pay vehicle excise duty, or to wear a helmet. Different laws apply outside the EU.

Electric power can also be handy off-road.

How long does the battery last?

This varies hugely according to the terrain, the size of the battery, and how much pedal effort you put in. Expect at least 20 miles, though some big batteries can manage 60 miles or more, and some manufacturers claim over 100 miles (see page 37).

How long do they take to charge?

Again, it depends on the battery size, as well as the charger: it can be anything from two to eight hours. You can always give the bike a shorter 'top-up' charge over lunch, or at work.

Are electric bikes safe?

Yes. The evidence shows that electric bike riders are no more likely to suffer

On many bikes batteries are neatly enclosed in the frame.

Extra loads can be carried with ease.

accidents than pedal cyclists, and better acceleration means they're less at the mercy of traffic (see page 12).

Are they heavy?
Electric bikes do weigh more than the equivalent pedal cycle, but this weight penalty is reducing as battery and motor technologies improve and these components become lighter. Current bikes weigh between 10 and 30 kilograms.

How fast can I go?
With power assistance, the legal speed limit is 15.5mph. You can, of course, ride faster than that without power assistance (given a downhill stretch or a tailwind).

Electric bikes don't recharge when braking or going downhill.

Well-equipped city/leisure bike, with lights, mudguards, rack, and a good range of gears.

Do they recharge going downhill or braking?

No. The returns are too small. Regenerative braking is worthwhile on an electric car, because of its weight and momentum, but not (with current technology) on an electric bike.

Isn't it 'cheating'?

No. By the same token, surely a modest family car is 'cheating' on a far bigger scale. On an electric bike, at least you're putting in some effort.

3 Why buy an electric bike?
– the benefits of making the leap

Some owners do have a sense of humour: this bike is powered by Guinness.

There are many good reasons for buying an electric bike, whether you're looking at a year-round commute, some gentle leisure cycling, or leaping along rocky mountainside tracks. Maybe you live in a very hilly area and just want a bit of help! Whatever the reason, there's probably an electric bike to suit you. There are pitfalls to buying, which we'll come to later, but here are the eight best reasons for going electric.

1. Supercharge your legs

Let's start with the most obvious advantage. An electric bike with a 250W motor will more than double your leg-power (unless you're Tour de France winner Sir Bradley Wiggins), making hillclimbs easy. You'll still notice hills, but a good electric bike with a decent set of gears will enable you to climb some very steep gradients indeed; a real boon if you live in a hilly part of the world. The same goes for that other bugbear for pedal cyclists: headwinds. These can make cycling a misery, but with an electric boost they are much less of an issue.

At a glance, some electrics could be mistaken for pedal cycles.

Pedelecs make efficient town transport.

Electric mountain bikes can be a lot of fun.

The extra power improves safety in traffic.

2. They're safer

Even though electric bikes can maintain higher average speeds than pedal cycles, they're also safer in traffic. The extra acceleration allows for faster hill starts and rapidly pulling away from busy junctions. Because you're picking up speed more quickly, the speed differential with traffic is less, so cars behind you effectively approach more slowly. Hillclimbing is safer for the same reason.

3. Cheap to run

Electric bikes are not cheap to buy, generally costing several hundred pounds more than the equivalent pedal cycle. However, once that upfront cost is out of the way, running costs are very low. The cost of a recharge is tiny (a few

A well-equipped pedelec will happily go touring.

Add a front basket to make it the perfect city bike.

pennies for a medium sized battery), and most of the components are standard cycle parts: things like tyres, cables, and brake pads, which last well and aren't expensive to replace. The only significant cost is the battery, which will have to be replaced every few years at ●x300-500.

4. The cycle advantage

Because electric bikes are – legally speaking – bicycles, they can use cycle paths, bridleways and cut throughs that are

Recharges cost a few pence.

closed to anything with an engine. They can park at cycle stands, or any odd corner where they're not in the way, just like a bicycle. Faced with a 'No Entry' sign, you just hop off and walk alongside your bike, which instantly turns you into a pedestrian.

Park at any cycle stand.

Pedelecs can use shared-use pedestrian/cycle paths.

5. No sweat

The prospect of turning
up at work all sweaty is
really off-putting for many,
especially in the summer,
when cycle commuting
should be at its most
pleasant. Working less
hard on an electric bike,
you should be less sweaty
as well.

6. Keep fit

Riding electric bikes
requires less effort than
bicycles, but they will still
help keep you fit. You
still have to pedal (except
on some older bikes
with separate throttles)
and most bikes have a
choice of power levels,
so you can turn down the
assistance level, or even
off altogether, if you feel
like a bit more exercise.
There's also evidence
that electric bikes get
used more often than
pedal cycles, potentially
because they actually
encourage owners to
leave the car at home and
get some exercise.

7. Resale value

Electric bikes tend to
hold their value well, so
if you do decide that
they're not for you, it
should be possible to sell
the bike for a reasonable
price.

Pedelecs keep you fit.

Greater towing capacity is another reason for buying an electric bike.

8. Sustainability

Not everyone is bothered about being green, but there's no denying that an electric bike is one of the most efficient forms of transport out there. The electricity has to come from somewhere, of course, but the associated emissions will still be minuscule compared to running a car, or even a small petrol scooter. If you have PV solar panels on your roof, charging your electric bike during daylight hours can make it a truly sustainable form of transport.

PV panels offer the prospect of recharging your pedelec with solar power: it's free energy.

4 The law
– keeping up with rules and regulations

In the UK and EU, electric bikes are treated the same as pedal cycles, in law, as long as the motor produces no more than 250W continuous power, and the bike won't exceed 15.5mph with power assistance. The bike must have pedals capable of propulsion, and the speed limit can be exceeded as long as the motor isn't helping. In practice, some bikes still give some assistance up to 18mph or so, but in a world where every car on the market can easily exceed the national speed limit, who's counting?

In other countries, the legislation varies. In the USA, federal law permits bikes up to 750W and 20mph assisted speed, though this can vary from state to state. Throughout the EU, the minimum riding age is 14 and there's no need for a licence. Helmets are not compulsory, though most manufacturers do recommend them.

To be road-legal in the EU, pedelecs must comply with power and speed limits.

Some EU countries have a special class for faster 'speed' pedelecs.

17

Faster electric bikes

If the bike is faster or more powerful than the limits stated previously, then it's classed as a moped. In the UK, this means you'll need insurance, an MoT, and vehicle excise duty (though this is free for an electric vehicle), and wearing a helmet is compulsory. The rider needs to be at least 16 years old, and possess a moped CBT qualification or a car licence with moped entitlement.

From 1st January 2017, these 'speed pedelecs' are confirmed as being in the moped category, but it's up to individual EU countries as to how to apply this law (also see page 33).

The minimum riding age in the EU is 14, allowing youngsters to have powered transport.

Electric bike power and speed restrictions also apply to public rights of way off-road.

Are they legal off-road?

Yes, but the same power and speed restrictions apply just as much for off-road public rights of way – that is, on bridleways, cycle paths and common land – as on the road. An electric mountain bike ridden on a muddy public right of way is still required to comply with the law to qualify as a bicycle. It's only when riding on private land, with the landowner's permission, that no power or speed restrictions apply.

Anywhere pedal bikes can go, electric bikes can go, too.

Motors are mounted in the hub (as seen here) or on the crank: this one has given eight years' reliable service.

Recent changes

There were some changes to EU law in 2015/16, with a 40kg maximum weight limit lifted in April 2015.

Until 1st January 2016, electric bikes could be sold with a throttle (either a twistgrip or thumb throttle) which allowed them to be ridden without pedalling. On bikes sold since then, the throttle can produce power only while the rider is pedalling, except up to walking pace. This is a useful feature, which enables you to walk alongside the bike up steep hills or while the battery is low. Bikes that are still able to throttle up to 15.5mph independently of pedalling now need to be type approved: this is something required of the manufacturer, and the importer or shop should know whether it's been performed.

None of this legislation is retrospective, and so it's not applicable to bikes sold before the new laws came in.

A word on power

Finally, a word on power outputs. Electric motors are often quoted as

More powerful motors are bigger: this is a 1000W Cyclotricity.

Some higher spec bikes – like this Benelli – look high-performance, but have the same power/speed restrictions as more conservative bikes.

A separate throttle or twistgrip (as seen here) can only supply power while the rider is pedalling, except at walking pace.

Electric motors have two quoted power outputs: the 250W limit refers to the maximum continuous power.

having two different maximum power outputs, both measured in watts. Maximum *continuous* power refers to power that the motor can keep producing all day: this is the 250W limit specified by law. Maximum *peak* power, on the other hand, is a higher figure which indicates what the motor can produce for a short time. So, a bike quoted as 250W will be capable of short bursts of power beyond that figure.

Good lights drain the main battery only a little, and well worth having.

The extra power of a pedelec can give confidence in traffic.

www.velocebooks.com/www.veloce.co.uk
Details all current books • New book news • Special offers • Newsletter

5 Choosing an electric bike
– which model for you?

The market for electric bikes has boomed in the last few years, and so has the choice of machines available to buyers. There are now electric mountain bikes, sporty road bikes, and cargo machines, to go alongside the practical commuter bikes.

The nitty-gritty

All electric bikes have the same basic components: they are a pedal cycle with the addition of an electric motor and battery. As such, they're a true hybrid, combining human and electric power.

The battery may be found behind the seat post, under the luggage rack, or (on more expensive bikes) smoothly integrated into the frame. In nearly all cases, it is removed for charging, which can be powered by any domestic supply using the charger supplied with the bike.

The motor may be mounted in the front or rear wheels (hub motor), or around the pedal cranks (crank drive). Until recently, the crank drive was restricted to higher priced bikes, but it's now

The battery is the heart of any electric bike.

Front hub motor used in the Nano Brompton conversion.

Motors are simple and rarely go wrong.

Some more comprehensive displays show battery charge, speed, distance ridden and assistance level.

becoming more widely available. A crank drive is more efficient than a hub motor, as it drives through the bike's own gear system.

Although the basic components are simple, modern electric bikes with lithium-ion batteries make increasing use of electronics to monitor the battery's performance and wellbeing – this is the Battery Management System (BMS).

All bikes have some sort of indication of battery level, from

If you don't have a full display, a basic cycle computer is still useful to keep an eye on battery range.

a simple light display on the handlebar switch to a more sophisticated digital display. Some level indicators can dip alarmingly when climbing a steep hill, only to 'recover' once you're going down the other side, so don't rely on them completely. They are still a useful tool, just remember that they give the most accurate indication when cycling steadily on a flat road. Manufacturers' claims regarding range can often be optimistic, and only your own experience with your own bike will reveal how many miles you can expect.

Electric bike technology has improved greatly in recent years. Early bikes in the mid-1990s were simple machines, using lead-acid batteries that were cheap but very heavy, and the bikes themselves were often made in China using low-cost components. Now there's a whole range of sophisticated European-made bikes, while many originating in the Far East have dramatically improved in quality. Which bike suits you best will depend on the kind of riding you want to do and, of course, how much you can afford to spend.

Hub motors have internal gearing to suit the wheel.

Commuter/touring bikes

These are the most common type of electric bike currently available, and usually come fully equipped with integrated lights (powered from the bike's own battery), full mudguards, and luggage rack. If you want to use the bike all year round, it should have all this equipment as a matter of course. Cheaper bikes tend to use hub motors, while the more expensive ones use crank drives. Although designed for road use, these bikes are also able to tackle gravel tracks and cycle paths.

A well-equipped commuter/tourer will be a pleasure to ride over longer distances.

Most bikes offer the choice of step-through or crossbar frames (or what used to be termed 'gents' and 'ladies'), but men shouldn't be put off by a 'ladies' frame: they're just as strong as the crossbar type for anything short of mountain biking, and are easier to hop on and off, especially for those of limited flexibility.

Gears are either hub or the more common derailleur: derailleurs are generally cheaper and offer a bigger choice of gears, while hub gears seal the cogs in a weatherproof hub. If you're commuting or riding all year round, go for hub gears.

Typical brands: EBCO, Freego, Momentum, Kalkhoff

Price range: ●x700-3000+

A step-through frame, chain guard, full mudguards, and a luggage rack all make life easier.

Pedelecs are fast becoming a regular feature of European city life.

Good commuter/touring pedelecs enclose the chain, sprockets and motor.

Road bikes

Electric road bikes are the sporty option. They're not quite Tour de France material, but you'll find them lighter and more responsive than a typical roadster; Cytronex claims to offer the lightest full-size electric bike on the UK market, weighing in at 12.7kg. Batteries tend to be small, which keeps the weight down but restricts range, and are often disguised as a water bottle or integrated into the frame.

The UK-assembled Cytronex is a good example of a lightweight

Light and nippy Cytronex racer: the 'water bottle' is actually a disguised battery.

Benelli Misano typifies the lighter, sportier style of pedelec.

cycle, with a water-bottle style battery and small front hub motor, based on a GT, Cannondale, or Merida road bike. The Benelli e-Misano, launched in 2016, has the battery built into the frame.

Typical brands: Cytronex, Benelli

Price range: ●x1350-3000

Mountain bikes

Electric mountain bikes are one of the fastest growing sectors of the pedelec market, and they make a lot of sense. The electric motor can help you up steep gradients and through tough patches, leaving you to enjoy the downhill stretches and easier tracks. What's more, mountain bikers seem less inclined to label electrics as 'cheating' than road riders.

Don't try this at home ... go into the mountains and do it there!

Fat bikes are hard work to ride on tarmac, unless you've got electric help.

Beware of lighter duty hybrids that are really just suited to gravel tracks: an electric mountain bike should have the battery very securely mounted, with wiring well protected from water and mud. The range of prices is huge, starting with the Cyclotricity Revolver from ●x700, a fairly basic bike with front hub motor. At the other end of the scale are premium bikes from KTM, the well known off-road motorcycle manufacturer, and Haibike, which is made in Germany. Prices for these start at around ●x2500, and reflect the specification, which includes top-grade frame, suspension, disc brakes, and crank-drive motors. The Spanish Bultaco Brinco is a faster option: more of a halfway house towards becoming a motorcycle, and offered in 28mph and 40mph versions.

Typical brands: Cyclotricity, Haibike, KTM
Price range: ●x700-8000+

Spanish-made Riejus are good-quality mountain bikes.

Bultaco Brinco is halfway between a mountain bike and a small motorcycle.

Retro Francis-Barnett apes the style of old British cycles:
period dress is not compulsory!

Cruisers and classics

If cruising along a breezy seafront and stopping off at an outdoor cafe sounds more appealing than climbing mountains, then a cruiser might be a better fit. These are long-wheelbase bikes that look like something out of 1920s New York (if you half close your eyes). Then there's the Francis-Barnett, which evokes 1950s delivery bikes. Both have all the usual pedelec components.

Typical brands: Francis-Barnett, Italjet

Price range: ●x1000+

Cruiser pedelecs such as this Italjet
could be perfect for promenading.

The Francis-Barnett looks as if it's come straight out of the 1950s,
but it's a modern pedelec.

Folding bikes

Electric folding bikes, for the most part, tend to be the cheapest models in a manufacturer's range, which shows up in the smaller batteries and sometimes lower quality. The biggest disadvantage of these cheaper folding electrics, which are offered for as little as ●x500, is their weight. This can be 25kg or more, which is a literal pain to lift into the boot of a car, or down into a boat. At 14in, the smallest wheels are less stable, and fat, low pressure tyres reduce the bike's efficiency.

The best electric folders are compact enough to fit into
the boot of a small car.

The Nano Brompton is one of the best folding bikes: the battery is hidden in the front luggage bag.

However, a few folding electrics are far lighter and easier to carry, while still folding down to a compact size. The Batribike V'Lec, launched in 2016, claims a weight of just 10.6kg, and costs ●x999. The ultimate electric folding bike is the Nano, a conversion kit for the well-established Brompton, with the small battery fitting neatly into the Brompton's luggage bag.

Typical brands: Viking, Nano

Price range: ●x500-2000

Cargo bikes

More commonly seen on the streets of Holland and Denmark, cargo bikes and trikes are a natural fit for electric power, given their capacity for heavy loads. Most of them take the form of trikes, with the cargo box sitting between two front wheels (see opposite page), and could be a good option if you often have to transport big loads or a gaggle of small children. They're not cheap, however, and

Electric folders have smaller wheels than full-size bikes, and step-through frames.

Family transport? The UK-made Boxer offers a fun alternative to more traditional options.

Electric cargo trikes make a striking statement for urban businesses and local deliveries.

take up a lot of garage room. They may look like fun, but a standard bicycle trailer is a cheaper option.

Typical brands: Boxer, Babboe

Price range:
● x2000-7000

Speed pedelecs

Speed pedelecs are bikes capable of more than 15.5mph, with some able to reach speeds of 25-28mph: as fast as a 50cc moped. In Germany, Holland, and Switzerland, a specific class for these bikes has been created, requiring insurance and a number plate.

The lightweight Cytronex isn't a speed pedelec, but it rides like one.

As mentioned elsewhere in this book, speed pedelecs are not legal for road use in the UK unless they have been registered, taxed and insured as a moped. The same applies to high powered electric bike kits fitted to pedal cycles, if it exceeds the 15.5mph/250W limits.

At the time of writing, speed pedelecs are on sale in Britain, and some importers claim they are legal if they can be switched between 250W and higher power modes.

The home-built Pagan from the UK is capable of over 50mph.

The M55 Terminus is fast and expensive.

However, the latest advice from the Department for Transport (November 2015) states that this doesn't count: the bike will be classed according to its higher power mode, and the ability to switch to a 250W mode doesn't make it legal.

As this book went to press, it was still not clear how the British government would implement a new EU directive, effective from 1st January 2017, which places all speed pedelecs into the moped class. As a directive, it gives national governments some leeway as to how it will be applied.

Typical brands: Cyclotricity, Kalkhoff

Price range: ●x1100-3500

It might look like a standard bike, but this Kalkhoff will achieve 28mph.

Online or in person?

It's very easy to buy an electric bike online, and there are some well-established online shops that specialise in electrics: you can find their details in the Useful Contacts section (see page 58). The problem, as with buying anything online, is what to do if something goes wrong.

Before buying, remember to check the small print, and find out what procedure the shop has in place for warranty work. Be sure that if you have to send the bike back under warranty, the shop will pay for the carriage. If the shop cannot be contacted by phone, or doesn't accept personal visits, buy elsewhere.

Buying face-to-face from an electric bike dealer means your choice of bike is ultimately limited to the dealers you're prepared to travel to. On the other hand, you can't overestimate the advantage of talking to a real person, and actually test-riding the bike you're interested

A knowledgeable dealership is the best place to buy a bike.

A few specialist pedelec dealers now exist.

Find a dealer that has been selling electric bikes for some time.

Buying online is easy, but local dealers
have their advantages, too.

in buying. Purchasing from a local dealer also means that it's easier to take the bike back and get it sorted out should something go wrong.

What size battery?

Battery capacity is crucial to an electric bike. It's akin to the size of a fuel tank: the more energy you can carry around with you, the further you can ride.

Capacity is measured in watt/hours (Wh). Not all manufacturers quote the battery size in Wh, but most do list the voltage (V) and amp/hours (Ah), allowing you to work out the Wh by multiplying voltage with Ah. So, a 36V battery of 10Ah has a capacity of 36 x 10, totalling 360Wh.

This still doesn't tell you how many miles the battery will provide power for, but you can make an educated guess. According to *A to B magazine*, power

consumption ranges from
an efficient 8Ah/mile to a
gas-guzzling 32Ah/mile,
with further variables
including the rider, terrain,
and weather conditions.

Let's assume
a consumption of
15Wh/mile. At this rate,
a 150Wh battery should
give a range of about ten
miles, a 300Wh battery
20 miles, and so on. In
practice, only the cheaper
bikes offer batteries of
less than 300Wh, and a
battery of 400-500Wh
gives a far more usable
range. A good guide is to
buy a battery that should
cope with at least double
your daily mileage. And
finally, don't rely on the
manufacturer's mileage
claims – they're usually
optimistic!

Warranty

The warranty is also vital,
because the battery is by
far the most expensive
component to replace if it
develops a fault. Ideally,
it should have a two-
year warranty, which is
becoming the norm on
bikes costing more than
●x1000.

Whatever the length
of warranty, read the small

**Unless restricted to
short distances, look for
the biggest, best quality
battery you can afford.**

print to find the point at which a claim can be made. Batteries rarely fail suddenly, but rather lose capacity over time, manifesting in a shorter operational range. The importers differ in how they measure this. Freego deems that a battery has failed if it has lost over 30% of its capacity, while Cyclotricity's definition applies to a battery once the range is down to six miles. If you have to make a claim and the dealer or importer disputes it, ask an independent auto

A good two-year warranty should give some peace of mind.

electrician to measure the capacity. More expensive bikes will have diagnostic plug-ins, which prove the battery condition beyond doubt.

Some manufacturers quote the expected life of the battery in charge cycles, usually listing them between 1000-1500 charges. However, this is not a warranty and, like range claims, can be optimistic. A good quality battery should last five to six years, if well looked after (see pages 45-49).

They are certainly fun, but this can turn sour if a failure occurs outside of warranty.

Pedelecs do weigh slightly more than conventional bikes.

Other than the foregoing there's not too much to worry about, apart from wiring and connectors: poor connections are simple to correct but difficult to diagnose. Electric motors are fairly simple components which rarely go wrong, while cycle parts such as brakes, gears, and tyres are well proven, and easily replaced by most cycle shops.

Some lighter bikes have become available since this Giant Lafree first came on the market.

Weight

While it's true that electric bikes are far lighter than they used to be, they still weigh more than the equivalent pedal cycle. A conventional cycle suitable for shopping or commuting will tip the scales at about 15kg, while the equivalent electric will weigh five to ten kilograms more. This is worth bearing in mind if you often have to haul the bike up steps, or onto a car cycle rack, though removing the battery will make this easier.

Shimano is one of the best known names in cycling,
so its power system should be trustworthy.

The name game

There are now many well-established
brands of electric bike, and many in the
UK have been in business for five years
or more, specialising in electric bikes,
rather than seeing them as a sideline.
It makes sense to choose a brand that
has some history in the area.

As for the electrical components,
drive systems from Bosch, Panasonic,
Yamaha, Shimano, and Impulse are all
safe bets, as are Samsung batteries,
though their quality is reflected in the
price. At the cheaper end of the market,
Bafang is a well established brand.
Of course, an unbranded cheaper battery
or motor could still give years of reliable
service, but it's a case of balancing risk
against what you can afford.

**A 'Made in Germany' badge will
impress many buyers.**

Piaggio, better known as the maker of Vespa scooters, launched a range of pedelecs in 2015.

The wish list
So, what should you look for in an electric bike?

Weight: Less than 25kg
Price: Expect to pay at least ●x1000 for a quality bike
Range: At least 25 miles (more if relying on manufacturers' claims)
Power consumption: Less than 10 watt/hours per mile
Warranty: Two years
Battery type: Lithium-ion or nickel-metal hydride
Battery price: Expect to pay ●x300-500 for a quality lithium-ion battery

7 Electric bike kits
– converting your current cycle

Electric kits are especially popular to retro-fit onto mountain bikes.

If you don't want to buy a complete electric bike, and especially if you already have a decent bike that fits you well, a conversion kit might be the answer. Although kits can be fitted by a competent home mechanic, this work is best entrusted to a cycle shop, and preferably the one you buy the kit from. If buying a kit online, check that your local bike shop is happy to fit it for you.

Most kits consist of a new wheel with hub motor, battery, pedal sensor, and all the associated wiring. Some may also include a digital display and brake cut-out switches.

The Cyclotricity kit fitted to this Dawes cycle obviously pleases the owner!

Cyclotricity electric bike kit parts, from top left: 1. controller; 2. keys; 3. brake levers (with cut-out switches); 4. display; 5. throttle; 6. pedal sensor; 7. battery; 8. battery cover; 9. new front wheel with motor and wiring.

Electric bike kits typically come with all the components you'll need for a conversion.

Much of the advice regarding buying a complete electric bike also applies when looking at conversion kits. Quality varies, so buy the best kit you can afford. Look for a two-year battery warranty, and try to buy from a local dealer rather than online. All the laws pertaining to electric bikes apply equally to conversions: the power and speed restrictions are the same, and in the EU converted bikes can only be ridden by those aged 14 and above.

8 Looking after an electric bike
– the importance of care and maintenance

An electric bike is a relatively simple machine – certainly compared to a car – but it will still respond to being cared for. As such, there are ways of maximising its lifespan, especially for the all-important battery.

An aftermarket high capacity battery with 720Wh – enough for nearly 100 miles of riding.

Battery types

Nearly all new electric bikes use either lithium-ion batteries or the very similar lithium-polymer: the names are often shortened to li-ion and li-pol respectively. The only exceptions at the time of writing are the Cytronex range, which use nickel-metal hydride, and a few much cheaper bikes (less than ●x600) that have continued with lead-acid batteries. Lead-acids are very heavy and provide a shorter life than other types, though they can easily be recycled and are by far the cheapest option. Some older bikes, such as the Giant Lafree, also use nickel-metal hydride batteries.

Other than these, lithium-ions have become universal, mainly because they're lighter and more compact than any other type of battery. Lithium-ions are well proven, having been found in small devices such as laptops and cameras for many years, and more recently branching out to electric cars as well as countless other devices.

Lithium-ion batteries have become almost universal.

Batteries remove easily for charging.

There have been a few instances of li-ion batteries overheating and actually catching fire, but this is very rare. To prevent this, they are fitted with a Battery Management System (BMS): a printed circuit board that can turn off any cells which are in danger of overheating. The BMS really is like a manager, keeping an eye on various parameters – battery voltage, temperature, and current – and protecting the battery by preventing it from overheating, overcharging, or discharging too far.

Battery care & charging

Every electric bike comes with a specific charger designed for its battery, and all of these will automatically switch off once the battery is fully charged. Some chargers for nickel-metal hydride batteries also have a 'refresh' facility, which will fully discharge the battery before commencing a recharge. This helps keep the battery cells in balance and charged at the same rate. If the charger has this facility, it should be

Always use the correct charger for the battery.

Keep an eye on the battery level display, and recharge before it gets too low.

used roughly once a month, but remember the whole process will take longer than a straight recharge.

Whichever type of battery your electric bike is fitted with, some basic tips can be followed to help to extend its lifespan:

Use the original charger: only use the charger that came with the bike. Attempting to charge (for example) a lead-acid battery with a charger designed for lithium-ion will cause damage to both.

A happy, fully-charged battery.

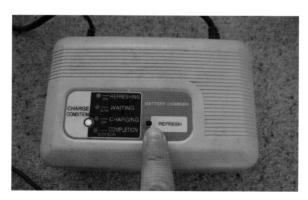

Some chargers have a 'refresh' facility to rebalance the battery cells.

Avoid charging overnight: although the risk of overheating is extremely small, it's safer to only charge batteries during the daytime, while someone is in the house.

Keep it part-charged: if the battery is left unused for long periods of time, give it a charge every couple of weeks to keep it about 50% charged. Lithium-ion batteries shouldn't be stored fully charged, or flat.

Don't completely flatten it: lithium-ion batteries in particular are not designed to run down until they're flat. As a result, it's a good rule to always recharge when the battery meter reaches its last segment, or the warning light comes on. If this happens on the road, just top it up for an hour or so: whatever is needed to get you home.

Baby it's cold: batteries are like humans; they don't like getting cold! Really cold weather will actually reduce a battery's operational range. To combat this, on sub-zero nights before an early start, make sure to keep the battery indoors overnight, and refit it to the bike only when you're about to set off.

9 Buying secondhand
– affordable, or a money pit?

If you feel you can't afford a new electric bike, there's a selection on the secondhand market that's growing as sales increase. Some importers, such as Powacycle and 50 Cycles (the Kalkhoff UK importer), offer secondhand bikes on their websites. Independent websites such as www.atob.org.uk and www.pedelecs.co.uk also have classified ad sections with bikes for sale. Sites such as Gumtree, eBay, and Craigslist are also worth keeping an eye on, as are your local newspapers: these won't have the same range of bikes to choose from, but they will be closer to home.

**An eight-year-old Kalkhoff with a nearly-new battery:
this should give many more years of service.**

What to look for

If you've read this far, you'll know that battery condition is crucial to an effective electric bike, especially secondhand. Ask the seller how much range he/she typically gets from the bike, though of course there's no way of verifying this without testing it yourself. Many used bikes come with a spare battery: a real bonus that will save money in the long term.

Older bikes, such as this Giant, should be cheap to buy.

For some older bikes, such as the Giant Lafree, new batteries are no longer available from the manufacturers. However, some specialist shops do offer a battery refurbishment service, which can be beneficial as long as the battery is in a fit state to be refurbished, which is not guaranteed.

One thing you don't need to worry about is the state of the cycle parts: the gears, brakes, tyres and cables. These are all standard components, available at all cycle shops, and relatively simple and cheap to replace if needed. So don't be put off by well worn tyres, rims, or brake blocks, though they can all be used to negotiate a lower price!

10 On your bike
– living with your new purchase

So, whether it's new or secondhand, you've bought an electric bike. What's next?

Riding techniques

In the FAQ section (see page 7), we mentioned that an electric bike is as simple to ride as a conventional pedal cycle, but it does have a couple of extra controls. On bikes with a separate throttle, it may take a little while to get used to how the bike responds, but that's just a case of practice.

Nearly all new bikes don't have throttles: the power just comes in automatically once you

It really will give you supercharged legs.

This is a 10% gradient, but she's sailing up it.

start pedalling, which
makes them simpler to
ride. Almost all electric
bikes have an on/off
switch located on the
handlebars. The exception
to this is the Cytronex
range; power comes on
when you press a 'boost'
button, and switches
off when you press the
button again or use the
brakes. Some bikes also
have an 'ignition' key as a
security feature.

Most bikes without
throttles also provide a
choice of power levels
– usually three or five –
which enables you to
select higher power for
climbing hills or battling
through headwinds. This is
a very useful tool, both for
making the ride easier and
for maximising your range.

For instance, when
approaching a hill, select
extra power before the
bike starts to slow down
to keep up momentum.
At the top, turn down the
power again to save a lot
of energy and increase
the range of your bicycle.
In busy stop-and-start
traffic, a higher power
level is useful for pulling
away safely from traffic
lights or junctions. Be
sure to experiment with
this, as not everyone is
comfortable with using a
higher power setting from
a standstill.

**If there's a choice of power levels, use them
to avoid wasting power.**

You might even find that you can turn off the power altogether on flat surfaces, and just rely on the power of your legs. Some bikes may require you to stop pedalling momentarily as you turn on the power again. Of course, with pedal power alone you'll be hauling the extra weight of the motor *and* battery, but it's nice to know the power is there when you need it.

What happens with a flat battery?

Batteries do not flatten suddenly and with no warning, so you're unlikely to become stranded miles from anywhere. Keep an eye on the battery gauge and/or warning lights, and over time experience will tell you how many miles you've got left when the indicators report low charge. Some bikes will also produce less power when the battery is this low. Eventually, the bike's power may cut out on a hill, but then recover after a little while and be operational on the flat. If you experience this, and you're a few miles from home, switch off the power and only switch it back on when you really need it. Try using the lowest power setting, which might help eke out the power just enough to get you home. As mentioned earlier, it's better for a lithium-ion battery's health not to let it get to this stage, and to recharge once the indicator reaches that last segment/light.

Careful riding should give you another few miles of power.

If the worst happens and you really do run out

Before setting out, check you've got enough power in the battery to get home.

of power, you can always pedal home. If that's too far, stop at a friendly pub, cafe, or service station, and ask if you can plug the battery in for 30 minutes while you have a coffee. It's an unusual request, but in the author's experience people are usually happy to oblige, as long as you buy something.

In fact, this ability to get home under your own power, or recharge anywhere with a domestic power supply, is one of the main advantages electric bikes have over other electric vehicles. They can charge nearly anywhere, and there's a backup power system in the form of your legs. In other words, there's no need for range anxiety!

Security

Like any bicycle, an electric will need to be locked when you park in a public place, especially as awareness grows that pedelecs are often more valuable than a pedal cycle. The same advice for keeping any cycle secure applies: buy a good quality lock, and secure the bike to an immovable object such as a bike stand or lamp post. Some Dutch-style bikes have a wheel lock built in, which is very handy and prevents the bike being wheeled away, though it could still be lifted into the back of a waiting van.

If you run flat, stop for a coffee and ask if you can charge the battery.

Some bikes have a convenient wheel lock, like this one, but a quality chain or U-lock is also a good idea.

Don't be afraid of venturing further afield than you would normally cycle.

Electric bikes are great for easy touring: just make sure you charge up every day.

However idyllic the destination, don't forget the charger (and the battery key)!

Further horizons

Now for the fun part! One of the best things about electric bikes is that they dramatically expand your cycling horizons. If you previously ran out of puff after five to ten miles, an electric bike can take you double the distance with only a little extra effort. New riders are often surprised by how much further they can travel and not feel tired at the end of a journey. Instead of carrying the cycles by car to a quiet road, you might be able to set off from home on the electric bike.

Cycle touring – going further afield and staying in a hotel or camping – is also made easier with an electric bike, especially with a higher capacity battery of 500Wh and above, enabling a daily mileage of 50 miles or more. There's a wide variety of good-quality cycle luggage available at any cycle shop, helping to make electric cycling a civilised experience. Just one thing: don't forget the battery charger and the key to remove the battery; without them you'll have an easy first day and a hard second one!

11 Useful contacts
– where to go for more information

This section lists some of the independent electric bike shops and sources of information in the UK. It's not a complete listing, so you may well find a specialist closer to you. All contacts were current at the time of going to press.

For a complete listing of electric bike importers and manufacturers, visit www.atob.org.uk/electric-bicycle-zone. This lists all UK importers/manufacturers, except those unable or unwilling to provide a UK phone number.

General websites/magazines
General cycle magazines, such as *Cycle* and *Cycling Plus* occasionally carry electric bike features and tests. *Watt Bike* is the only UK-based magazine devoted to electric bikes, as a supplement to *Twist & Go* magazine.

www.twistandgo.com
Watt Bike supplement for *Twist & Go* magazine.

www.atob.org.uk
A complete listing of bikes available, plus technical/legal advice.

www.pedelecs.co.uk
Wide ranging website with lots of advice and a forum.

Specialist shops
Banchory Cycles – Aberdeen (Volt only)
www.banchorycycles.com
01330 820011

Damian Harris Cycles – Cardiff
www.damianharriscycles.co.uk
02920 529955

E-Bike Shop – Hampshire
www.e-bikeshop.co.uk
01252 279279

E-Motion – Reading
www.e-motionevc.co.uk
01793 251200

Electric Cycle Centre Penrith – Cumbria
www.electriccyclecentrepenrith.co.uk
01768 864775

Electric Cycle Company – Edinburgh
www.electriccyclecompany.com
01315 520999

London Electric Bike Company –
London
www.londonelectricbike.com
07841 412199

North Yorkshire Electric Bikes –
Yorkshire
www.ny-ebikes.co.uk
01423 603423

The Electric Bike Shed – Tyne & Wear
www.theelectricbikeshed.co.uk
01914 274739

The Electric Bike Shop – Norfolk
www.electric-bike-shop.co.uk
01493 603388

The Electric Transport Shop – London,
Oxford, Cambridge, Bristol, York
www.electricbikesales.co.uk
01905 611774

Wirral Ebikes – Liverpool
www.wirralebikes.co.uk
01516 910006

Watt Bike **is the UK-based pedelec
magazine.**

The Essential Buyer's Guide™ series ...

Other titles from Veloce Publishing

Caring for your bicycle – Your expert guide to keeping your bicycle in tip-top condition
Peter Henshaw

With expert advice on how to adjust your bike to fit you, how to clean it efficiently, and how to keep it running in top condition, this guide lets you get more enjoyment from your bicycle for longer, more safely, and with the sense of satisfaction that comes from knowing you can fix or prevent problems that may arise yourself – you could even save yourself a small fortune in repair bills.

Paperback ISBN: 978-1-845844-77-6
21x14.8cm • £6.99* UK/$11.99* USA • 64 pages • 97 colour pictures

eBook ISBN: 978-1-845845-42-1
eV4542 • Flowing layout • 97 pictures •
Base price £4.99

How your motorcycle works – Your guide to the components & systems of modern motorcycles
Peter Henshaw

A fascinating and complex piece of machinery, the modern motorcycle is easily as complex as the modern car. Clear, jargon-free text, and detailed cutaway illustrations show exactly how the modern bike works.

Paperback ISBN: 978-1-845844-94-3
21x14.8cm • £12.99* UK/$25.00* USA • 80 pages • 86 colour pictures

eBook ISBN: 978-1-845845-37-7
eV4537 • Flowing layout • 86 pictures •
Base price £7.49

For more info on Veloce titles, visit our website at
www.veloce.co.uk • email: info@veloce.co.uk • Tel: +44(0)1305 260068
* prices subject to change, p&p extra

Other titles from Veloce Publishing

Funky Mopeds! – The 1970s Sports Moped phenomenon
Richard Skelton
A celebration of the sports moped charting the history of a genre created unwittingly by the government in 1972 and killed off by more legislation five years later. This book recaptures the spirit of happy and carefree times and looks at the bikes that gave freedom and mobility to a generation.

Paperback ISBN: 978-1-845840-78-5
25x20.7cm • £27.50* UK/$49.95* USA • 144 pages • 150 pictures

eBook ISBN: 978-1-845844-80-6
eV4480 • Flowing layout • 150 pictures • Base price £10.99

The A-Z of popular Scooters & Microcars – Cruising in style!
Mike Dan
An A to Z color reference book covering classic motor scooters and microcars primarily from the 1950s to the 1970s. A hugely entertaining "I was there" account of of the classic scooter and microcar era, this book is highly illustrated and also contains an essential A-Z reference to these fascinating machines.

Paperback ISBN: 978-1-845840-88-4
25x20.7cm • £15.00* UK/$59.95* USA • 256 pages • 441 colour and b&w pictures

eBook ISBN: 978-1-845848-75-0
eV4875 • Flowing layout • 441 pictures • Base price £10.99

For more info on Veloce titles, visit our website at
www.veloce.co.uk • email: info@veloce.co.uk • Tel: +44(0)1305 260068
* prices subject to change, p&p extra

Index